LIFE MANAGEMENT
- 100 PRINCIPLES

LIFE MANAGEMENT - 100 PRINCIPLES

Ketan Parekh

PARTRIDGE
A Penguin Random House Company

To order additional copies of this book, contact
Partridge India
000 800 10062 62
orders.india@partridgepublishing.com

www.partridgepublishing.com/india

Preface

Every building has four pillars. Whether it is my two storied house Shantiniketan or world's tallest tower Burj Khalifa. All pillars have equal importance. If we make one pillar strong and other pillar weak it is very risky and dangerous for the survival of any building or structure.

Similarly our life is also made up of four pillars. We have to make each pillar equally strong and has to give equal importance to make our life happy and successful. In our life the four pillars are- 1) Physical and Mental 2) Social and Emotional 3) Career and Finance and 4) Spiritual and humanity.

So to manage our life and to be happy and successful in our life, we have to manage all these pillars. Hence taking all the four pillars of our life, I have set 100 Principles to manage our life. So, the title of the book is "Life Management – 100 Principles". I hope you will find interesting to read and very practical to implement and wish you all success to manage your life happily and successfully.

Contents

C) Career and Financial Management

D) Spiritual and Humanity Life Management

A) Physical and Mental Life management

1) Live Fearless life

The first and foremost quality of life is to live the life without fear. Fear is nothing but gaining knowledge.

Knowledge can be gained by learning, reading and knowing.

The more you know, the less you fear

The more you learn, the less you fear

The more you read, the less you fear

It is said that the readers are leaders'. US President Bill Clinton read more than 300 books during his study at Oxford University. Try to read at least one good book a month. Get knowledge and information from all available resources. And use wonders of technology to gain knowledge about anything and everything to eradicate fear from life

Rabindra Nath Tagore wrote: Where the mind is without fear and the head is held high . . . . .

You will be winner in every field once you lose the fear of losing. Take charge of your life, otherwise somebody else will control and run your life.

2)   Do Exercise and Meditation regularly

Your body and mind remains with you till you are alive. Anybody can come in your life and anybody can go out of your life but your body and mind remains always with you in your lifetime. So it is our duty to give some time to our body and mind only without a disturbance

Try to give at least 30 minutes in the morning for exercise and yoga and 30 minutes before you go to bed for meditation

Pascal wrote all person miseries come from not being able to sit alone with himself quietly

By giving 30 minutes each to our body and mind, you will be able to unleash the hidden potential of it, can interact and extract much more for it like a mine

Doing regularly exercise and meditation will make you an all round complete person-guiding parents, successful leader, caring life partner, cooperating friend, and loving boss.

Those who believe they do not have time for exercise, must understand that sooner or later they will have to give time to sickness.

It is well documented that there is a direct correlation between fitness and not only your performance but also basic things like self esteem, self love and self acceptance.

3)   Relaxation of Mind, Body and Soul

There is a direct link between our body, mind and soul. If we relax our body and give enough rest to our body after work then our mind also get relaxed and cool down and think better and positive. Then when mind is thinking good and positive, our soul gets purified. Again if soul gets purified it give new strength to our body and energy to our mind. Spend minimum 30-45 minutes in the morning for your body, mind and soul. Do some physical exercise, workouts and stretching for body. Do some yoga for balancing our vital internal organs and relaxing our mind. Do some meditation and relaxation technique for inner peace of our soul. You can also listen music or some spiritual and motivational lectures to give food for thought. Your body, mind and soul remains with you till you die. So it is our moral duty to give some time for our body, mind and soul. Those who do not give such time eventually attracts illness.

Also remember, to double your speed, take a pause. Give rest to your mind and body.

Our body needs food, water and light everyday. Similarly our mind needs positive thoughts and relaxation everyday and our soul needs some deed of kindness and meditation to purify our inner soul.

4) Develop Healthy Diet and Food Habits

A healthy mind in a healthy body. So develop healthy diet and food habits and stay fit and healthy. Many youngsters ignores this and suffer at a later stage in life. All of you must be knowing the following healthy diet and food habits so I strongly urge you to follow that:

1) Drink minimum 2 litre of water
2) Take minimum oil, salt, sugar and junk food.
3) Take maximum salads, green vegetables, pulses and soups.
4) Take more staple food and fibre food
5) Take less fatty food
6) Eat regularly 3 fruits or drink juices
7) Take a glass of milk at least once in a day
8) Make your breakfast heaviest, lunch lighter, small snacks and dinner very light
9) Take curd, butter milk or lassi
10) Prefer vegetarian food

Also strictly implement the following hygienic habits:

1) Wash hands before taking food
2) Trim your nails regularly and keep it clean
3) Brush your teeth twice in a day
4) Never make your dining table your office table or reading table
5) Try to observe silence while taking food
6) Thank God every time you take food
7) Don't waste your food

5)   Control your mind by breathing

Mind is closely connected with breathing process. The prefect breathing process has the power to activate your subconscious mind and to control your conscious mind. It has the power to connect you to your soul and ultimate source of energy. Let me explain you in a simple way. Your breathing is quick and shallow when you feel tension and pressure. Your breathing is calm and deep when you are quiet and relaxed. You visually become breathless when you are in deep meditation

If you can control your mind you can control worst situation and also convert to the adverse situation in your favor. It is said that "To breathe correctly is to live correctly"

By preaching the art of breathing technique you can train your mind, frame your mind and even control your mind.

It is said that breath is fuel, breath is life and when you control your own breath nobody can make you sad or steal your peace.

I would strongly recommend you to attend Dr Sneh Desai's "Mind Power", a 2 day workshop whenever you get chance.

6) Eliminate Stress

Stress and tensions are silent killer. It damages our body, disturbs our social life by breaking relationship, leads our career and financial life at sixes and sevens (totally disorder and unorganized). So it is of utmost important to eliminate stress from our life if we want to live happily

A very simple technique of eliminating stress is to write the name of person or situation or thing which give us stress and than to burn the paper and flush out the ashes of burnt paper. The technique was shown in bollywood films "Jab we met". Even Bruce Lee used this technique often.

However some people who are well disciplined and focused use stress as a tool also. They use it to deliver their best overcome their limitation s to achieve something which seems impossible.

Never feel stress from your job as it is really bad for health. Stress draws you to bad habits like smoking, drinks, depressions etc

So many men and women carry tremendous physical demands and extended level of stress. Their bodies warn them several times before they have any big trouble.

7) Control anger

Aristotle thought "Anyone can become angry. That is easy. But to be angry with right person to the right degree at the right time, for the right person and in the right way is not easy."

Never develop anger as your habit which in the long term becomes your second nature. People with such habit has suffered a lot in the form of broken relationship, broken partnership etc and looses credibility. On the other hand people who remains calm and control anger in adverse situation are effective, successful and liked by all.

A simple method to control anger is to count 1-100 before speaking anything in hot situation. The scientific method to control anger is to pass your thought and words through three test before speaking because words like arrows-once releases can't be retrieved. The three test are:

1. Is it truth?
2. Is it necessary?
3. Is it kind?

Give up anger and control yourself before getting angry. It will empower you. Anger is a state of insanity because calmness is wisdom. Anger Management Tips-

1) Once you are calm, express your anger if still genuine.
2) Do some exercise.
3) Go for a timeout or break.
4) Identify alternative solution or situation.
5) Share a joke.
6) Relaxation and Meditation

Foolishness is the starting point of anger and it ends with lamentation. The size of man can be measured by the size of the thing that makes him angry. Holding on to anger is like keeping a burning piece of coal in your hands to throw at your enemy, but it burns you first. When new have the ability to listen to almost anything without losing our temper, we are truly educated. When you are right, there is no need to be angry. When you are wrong, you have no right to be angry. If you are patient in one moment of anger, you will escape a hundred days of sorrow.

8)   Tolerate pain

Whenever you get hurt or problem comes or troubled by something you get pain or become sad try to control or tolerate and absorb the pain

When you get cool analyze the situation that made you hurt or sad and learn something important from your bad experience

Take pain as blessing and consider it as a teacher like a failure is a stepping stone to success.

To hold tight, you have to loosen first.

Initially it takes an effort to smile in pain, then it becomes a habit, then over a time you win over your pain.

Do not hold. Learn to let go. It saves you from pain and can make someone happy.

A successful man is one who can lay a firm foundation with the bricks that others throw at him.

9)   Be alone and find your loneliness

I wish I could fly alone in the sky, spreading my wings with complete freedom. I could not. But then I started going deep with my thoughts and I am flying in the depth alone ever since.

To be able to lead others, a man must be willing to go forward alone.

Focus your attention within yourself and find yourself in a place inside you with total happiness, pure love, self acceptance and discover your self worth. Take a pause and learn how to remain standstill. Observe complete silence and stay with you and enter yourself within you for at least 15-30 minutes daily. Silence is powerful to awake you. Be alone and enjoy loneliness in complete silence. Switch off your thought process and feel the state of no mind by giving pause to your mind and just listen to your heart what he says and what he is talking to you. Silence is Golden and see your loneliness as a solitaire Diamond within you. Make loneliness as your best companion whenever you are alone. You will find the most appropriate and best answer to all your question from your within when you ask it alone in your loneliness. Spend time alone with yourself everyday.

You can also stand out and find your loneliness as a performer. From loneliness you can convert yourself from ordinary to extraordinary.

10) Let the Age Grow but be Young at Heart

Bollywood film actor Dev Anand lived for more than 80 years. He always used to say his age in terms of 20's like I am 20x4 years old

Dr L.F. Phelan said "You are as old as your doubt, your fear, your despair."

To remain young you have to keep your faith young, keep your self confidence young, keep your hope young.

Your skin wrinkle with time but heart never slows or reduces beats with time. So be young at heart even at the age of 60 or 70 or 80. You may look older in your appearance but always feel young with your heart.

It does not matter whether you are 18 or 81, stay fit, self motivated and be passionate about your life till last breath.

Never die mentally before you die actually. Never be old mentally till your last breath.

Age is an issue of mind over matter. If you don't mind, it does not matter.

Life's tragedy is that we get old too soon and wise too late.

11) Develop Attractive and Dynamic Personality

This does not mean that you should be beautiful or handsome, tall and slim, fair and sharp features. This mean you should develop good habit and etiquette. It may be good at public speaking, art of conversation, good and patient listener, personal grooming, dressing sense, following dress code, habit of socializing, witty nature, how to stand, your walking style, your eating habits and style, showing respect and courtesy, how to sit, your body posture, your body language, cleanliness etc. We all has the potential to do all these so we can set it as our goal.

Our body is the baggage we must carry throughout our life. The excess the baggage, the harder the journey and less enjoyable.

12) Develop 25 Habits

Success is simple and it is yours if you develop following 25 habits:

1) Dream More
2) Think High
3) Act confidently
4) Plan Perfect
5) Work Hard and Smart
6) Execute well
7) Learn and Grow
8) Be Positive
9) Healthy Food and Diet
10) Pray for All and Everyone
11) Talk Softly
12) Breathe Deeply
13) Exercise, Meditation and Yoga Daily
14) Sleep Less
15) Dress Smartly
16) Trust Cautiously
17) Earn Honestly
18) Save and Invest regularly
19) Spend Intelligently
20) Donate Before you Die
21) Set your Priorities
22) Connect with Nature and God
23) Give Mission to Your Life
24) Love Yourself
25) Be a good Parent

13) From Bed to Bed

Get up from bed when Sun gets up in your city. Do the following things after getting up:

1. Drink two glass of water
2. Spend 10 min for exercise,10 min for yoga and 10min for meditation
3. Do the routine and take nice hot water bath
4. Sit 15min in front of God-connect with him feel him and express your gratitude for this wonderful life
5. Go under the Sun, take fresh air and energy.
    Go to bed and sleep in between 10-11 pm
    Never watch TV or read anything while lying on your bed.

Do the following things before you go to bed and lie down?

1. Analyze your day and write down one good things and one bad thing happened and held yourself responsible for both
2. Take your meal at least 2 hrs before you go to bed
3. Play with a child 10 min before you go to bed
4. Meditate for 10min
5. Visualize your goal

Never go to bed with a grievance against anyone.

14) Sleep 6-7 Hours a day

As per the scientific study an adult person does require sound sleep of 6-7 hours daily to maintain good state of health. I sleep from 11pm to 5am from April to September and from 11p to 6am from October to March.

Remember it is the quality of sleep that is more energetic and refreshing to our body than quantity of sleep. If you are able to extract 1 hour more for your work out of your sleep, you get 30 hours a month or 365 hours per year extra and this time can contribute a lot in your start up career and for meeting deadline for any project. So to make your life more meaningful, productive and rewarding sleep not more than 6-7 hours a day. Believe me friends if you work 12 hours a day and sleep 6-7 hours a day upto the age of 45-55 years, then after that you can sleep for more than 12 hours in a day because by that time you must have achieved most of your goal.

15) Ailments, Disease and Disorder

We give power and energy to our body and we only consume power and energy of our body. We are responsible for running, maintaining and repairing our body and so we are also creator of illness in our body. Almost all diseases are created in our body by 4 most damaging acts of ours. These are- Anger, Stress, Guilt and Criticism.

Believe me friends giving up anger and releasing resentment can even cure cancer.

You can read the book "You can Heal Your Life" by Louis Hay in which you will find what thought pattern of our causes different diseases and also what are the remedial thought process to cure that diseases.

Buddha said every man is the author of his own health or disease.

Best doctor in the world: Sunlight, Water, Air, Exercise, Relaxation, Diet, Family and Self confidence.

In first half of our life we try to gain wealth and lose our health. In second half of our life we spend wealth to regain our health.

B) Social and Emotional Life Management

16) Enjoy with family

To spend time with family, for the family and on the family is the best use of time to make our social and emotional pillar of life strong.

By giving minimum30-60 minutes of time with family will give enough energy and enthusiasm to make your working hours most productive and fruitful

If possible try to take food together with whole family. It may be breakfast, lunch, dinner or even a cup of tea/coffee with snacks/biscuits. It is said that family who eats together stays together. Bonding with family gives happiness.

Try to spend Sunday with your family. This does not mean that for the entire day Sunday you remain at home and do your activities only like daily routine, taking long day sleep after lunch, watching late night TV, surfing internet and involved in social media sites etc. I mean you should spend quality time with each and every member of your family. You can help your spouse in removing clutters from wardrobe, kitchen or bathroom or in some cleaning activities, you should play with your child, talk with him or help him in his study, go out in the evening to a park, or watch a movie together and take dinner in a restaurant, even you can take help of your family members in some urgent and important work of yours.

Family, health, friends and spirit do not come with a price tag. But when we lose them, we realize the cost and the loss we incurred.

Always give quality time to your family, else one day you will have enough time but without family.

17) Know and Admire Great Qualities of Great People

People collect and stock pictures of their celebrity, super stars, great and successful businessman, body builders and fighters. Children and students keep collecting pictures of their favorite character or cartoons. But very few of them are aware that why their hero is so famous and what are their great qualities and characteristics. So one should know and admire qualities of their hero. In fact I would ask them to write the qualities of their hero and paste it below their pictures. Every day they should see the picture and read the qualities and follow and implement in their life. Very soon you will find that all those qualities is coming within you.

Some of the great qualities of the great people are:

1) Disciplined, organized, consistent, learning and action oriented
2) Focus on Money, Manage Risk, fully aware of income & expenses
3) No Negative Thoughts, negative feelings, enjoy life and work
4) Never greed, fear, guilt, jealousy. Big thinking and ambitions.
5) Kind, loving, sharing, forgiving, humble and attitude of gratitude
6) No arguments, blames, complain and criticism.
7) Perfect time management. Better listener and good speaker.
8) Physically fit with healthy diet and food habits and care their body
9) Strong networker, build relationship, quick and prompt decision
10) Sleep less, work more and take holidays/vacations regularly.

The quality of your life will improve if you accept, admire and apply the great qualities of great people.

18) Choosing Life Partner is the most Important Decision of Life

We spend normally two-third of our life with our spouse or life partner. So selecting and choosing spouse is the most important decision of life. I am of the opinion that we should choose our soul partner as life partner. Today's generation's young boys and girls started believing in this. They have new attitude towards marriage. They believe in simplicity and frankness, mutual trust and confidence, sharing of problems and difficulties, expressing of love and care for each other. They understand and be understood.

My inner conscious of heart is yet to give me approval for same sex marriage. So I cannot express any though on that.

There are some other factors also which can be considered while choosing your spouse. These are- care, affection, sense of humor, intelligence, integrity, family background, maturity, companions, temperament, cooperation, adjustability, frankness, flexibility. In short you have to judge your chemistry with your spouse. Never take hasty decision under pressure or compulsion.

Never settle for anybody for just to have someone. Set your own standard for choosing life partner. List the qualities you have and list of qualities you want to develop, you will attract the person with such qualities.

While choosing life partner for your life always make a clear demarcation between "what" you want in your life and "who" you want in your life.

19) Always support your spouse

Your spouse is known as your better half. So each of us is incomplete without our spouse. Hence you should always support your spouse and get the support of your spouse in whatever you do by sharing with your spouse. Also listen your spouse with attention and help your spouse. One should act as a fuel to fulfill the desires and dreams of each other. Physically both of you must be two but become one mentally and have coinciding thoughts, unanimous decision and unified action. This will create a lifelong strong bonding and will make both of yours life very happy. Love your spouse as much as you love yourself. Protect and take care of your spouse as much as you protect and take care of your body.

Most happy couples rarely have the same nature, character and understandings. They just make the best of their differences. Many times they agree to disagree on a point.

A single finger which wipes out your tears in your bad times is much better than ten fingers which join hands and clap in your victory.

We generally do not give attention to any part of our body till it pains, but never do that with your spouse. Give her love, care and attention all the time.

Failure also looks beautiful, when you have a loved one to support you. Success also hurts, when you do not have a loved one to wish you.

20) Always Forgive but Never Forget

Forgetting and ignoring your enemy means insulting your enemy which will create more ill feeling but forgiving him will earn a pride for you and he will feel good and chances are there that your enemy will become your friend. So develop the tendency of forgiving by forgetting the past. Never forget your enemy rather always remember him but never with ill feeling or bad experience. Remember with the willingness to forgive him to release the bad memory of past. Develop this attitude. So all you need to do is to express willingness to forgive and leave the rest to God and Universe to deal with it. I call this L S F G U – Leave Something For God and Universe.

Always remember forgiving is easier than to forget. Forgiving makes you feeling of freedom and makes you light.

Forgiving is a virtue that gives you peace of mind. To err is human, to forgive is divine.

Forgive when it is very difficult to do so.

One of the hardest thing to do in life is to forget whether it is guilt, anger, love lost etc You have to fight to remember and also to fight to forget.

By just saying three simple words "I Forgive You" lot of lives are enriched and lot of relationships are rebuilt much stronger than earlier. When we do not forgive in one relationship our love is restricted and mixed with bitter feelings in our other relationships also.

Forgiveness has nothing to do with whether someone deserves to be forgiven or not. It is simply an act of love and not of justice.

It takes a strong person to say sorry and even stronger person to forgive.

As long as we do not 'forgive' others, they occupy 'rent free' space in our mind.

21) Call People by Name and Appreciate them

People like when you call them by their name. They feel personalized and come closer to you when you remember their name and call by their name. You can quickly build rapport with a person when you call him by his name and also appreciate him. This is so because everyone in this world by natural instinct likes to feel distinguished by their name and feel happy when appreciated. This is a proven fact with even animals also because when a pet called by its name also feel excited. Almost all people love their name first.

People will forget what you said, people will forget what you did but people will always remember how you call them and what feelings you generate in him. If you create interest in other people by appreciating them you can make more friends rather than trying to get people interested in you. This is why people do not like to get imposed.

You may always try to prove yourself right but never attempt to prove that others are wrong. To be kind is more important than to be right; often people need a patient heart that listens, not a brilliant mind that speaks and give scores and make judgment.

Too often we underestimate the power of a touch, a small word, a listening ear, an honest compliment or the smallest act of caring- all of which have the potential to turn a life around.

22) Networking is smart socializing

Always meet new people and make friendship with them and increase your contacts. This is called networking. Networking is smart socializing because once you know the people from varied and diversified fields and areas you may get help from any such people if you are stuck up anywhere in your life. Moreover you can also be helpful by providing a reference of your friend to another person who may be requiring the product or services of your friend. Again wherever you will go, you will find some common friends so that you will never feel stranger. Networking is also a smart way of selling your product or services. One way of good networking is to give importance to the other person, focus on him, listen him and appreciate him. Try to avoid "I" and make more use of "YOU" and "WE" This will result in making friendship easy. You will make end number of friends if you give importance to every person you meet in this world.

23) Communicate Timely and Accurately to maintain Good relationship

Communication plays an important part in maintaining good relationship. In communication our body language has very important role to play when we are in meeting with one to one or in presence of many. Our voice and tonality is another important factor in communication. Tonality is how we speak. It creates an enormous difference in the meaning when we speak with different tonality. Listening is also a part of communication. Never give ignored listening to anyone. Give attentive listening when you are meeting one to one and give selective listening when you are in many. Timely response and reply is very important when you are away from someone. Moreover mode of communication is also very important in today's time. Reply with SMS if he is expecting SMS, reply with mail if he is expecting mail, give a phone call if he is expecting your call, meet the person if he wants to meet you. Moreover, in whatever mode you reply but it should be complete reply. You should answer/ explain all question/matter asked to you. So make a planned communication.

Communicating to people is somewhat similar to being a goalkeeper. No matter how many goals you save, people only remember the one you missed! The most important thing in communication is to hear what is not being said. The real art of conversation is not only to say the right thing in the right place, but also to leave unsaid the wrong thing at the tempting moment. It takes three years to learn how to speak but it takes lifetime to learn where, when, how and how much to speak. Never underestimate the power of your tongue. If not held tight and managed properly, this softest organ of your body could be responsible for the hardest phase of your life. Your success over a lifetime will be more directly linked to your writing and speaking skills.

24) Admit Your Mistakes and take Criticism with Positive Attitude

A man can become powerful in society and achieve enduring success and become big enough only when he held himself responsible and blame only himself for all mistakes and failures not only done or committed by himself but also by his team and subordinate.

So accept criticism with positive attitude and be open to feedback. Mistakes takes you to perfection so it is very important to admit your mistakes. Never try to neutralize your mistakes by twisting facts. You can learn from mistakes so mistakes are essential. Only mistakes and failures leads to success.

We get comfort from those who agree with us but we get growth and learning from only those who do not agree with us. The people who accept criticism are the people who are genuinely interested in self-improvement.

If someone feels that they had never made a mistake in their life, then it means they had never tried a new thing in their life. Competition and criticism are our partners for our improvement and growth. Always welcome them, thank them and bless them.

Many receive advice and criticism but only wise make best use of that to make profit from it. When someone criticizes us, it is time to evaluate ourselves. When someone praises us, it is time to evaluate them.

Some of the biggest problems arise when we begin to believe that we are perfect or that the world should be perfect.

25) Be a Good Parent

Commit yourself to be a good parent. Parent always do what is the best for their child so I am just mentioning what I follow:

1) Give your child the gift of freedom and awareness.
2) Install leadership qualities in your child from the beginning.
3) Cheer him up with great enthusiasm in whatever he does.
4) Help your child to make friends.
5) Teach your child how to respect and trust so that he never tell lie.
6) Help your child to overcome fear and phobia.
7) Spend quality time with your child because for them LOVE is your TIME. It is your greatest gift
8) Teach them tradition, make him understand the value and importance of rules, regulation and discipline and then let him to decide what and how to follow.
9. Stay united as parent and never quarrel and abuse each other in front of child.
10) Never beat the child
11) Pursue and explain your child instead of angry/scold
12) Never make comparison and grading between your children.
13) Never tease or threaten the child.
14) Teach your child about the value of money
15) Teach him how to take his own decisions.
16) Never pressurize your children to follow a particular career of your choice and never pressurize your children to marry a particular boy/girl
17) Never put the pressure of study all time.

In the Prophet, Khalil Gibran says: "Your children are not your children. They are the sons and daughters of Life's longing for itself." I am still making analysis on these to understand fully its meaning.

26) Avoid Arguments, Blames and Complain (ABC)

Avoid strictly – A- Arguments, B- Blames and C- complain.

It is injurious and harmful to health and wealth. This is a statutory warning and beneficial advice. Sometimes during an argument, if one stops arguing or fighting or stop proving a point, it may not mean that he is defeated or he loses. It may be so that he is holding the dignity of the other person higher than him. In short one should not always try to prove himself right in every situation and enter into arguments. One should try to understand other person's point of view and understand his circumstances.

Never play blame game and complain to cover up faults. Held yourself responsible for every situation and circumstances created for you, but never blame anyone for any situation or problem nor complain to anyone for any circumstance or obstacles. Stop blaming and complaining and start living by creating situation and circumstance suites for you.

Never condemn anything which you have not investigated. If you have genuine grievances express by writing it and then communicate. Avoid speaking it out loudly and in presence of everyone. We are responsible for all our acts and experience. So never waste time in arguing, blaming and complaining anyone.

The person who argues, blames, complains and criticize always look for negative in everything. They can never succeed in life.

The more arguments we win, the more friends we lose. A lot of trouble would disappear if people talk "to" one another instead of "about" one another.

Argument is bad. But discussion is good. Arguments find out 'who' is right. Discussions find out 'what' is right. One constructive suggestion is worth a hundred complains.

When we argue unnecessarily, we lose our power of judgment.

27) Never Think Loose and Discrete

What we Think says what we can Do.

What we Do converts us into what we Are.

What we Are says what we Think.

To control thoughts and to change the direction of your thoughts is the secret of all success on this planet. You have the power to do so with your thoughts and you have to use that power to make yourself successful.

You are the remote control of your mind. Never become slave of your mind but become master of your mind. Every thought is creating your future.

We are supported by the universe for all thoughts we choose to think and believe. The power of universe is great but it never judges or criticize our thoughts.

We have the power to choose our thoughts and capability to change our thoughts.

If you are cautious about extravagant spending and also use your time and energy for good causes then never waste your energy in loose thinking also. Control your thoughts, redirect your thoughts from negative to positive and you will see good things are happening in your life. You will feel more powerful and will be able to do difficult task easily.

Always accept the best and deserve the best thought. The trouble with most people is that they think with their hopes and fears, rather than with their minds.

The regrets we should have is not for the wrong things we did; but for the right things we could have done but never did. Be careful in your thoughts when you are alone and be careful in your words when you are in a crowd. If your eyes are sweet you will like all people of the world but if your thoughts are sweet, all people of the world will like you. Think before you speak, but never speak all you think.

28) Change with the Change and Flow with the Flow

By changing the flow of thoughts in your mind, you can change yourself and by changing yourself you can change the flow of thoughts in your mind.

Remember you are the captain of your ship LIFE and you have to sail your ship to harbor of success by changing the direction of ship with the change in the direction of wind and sail smoothly your ship with the flow of waves.

We believe in many rigid rules and believe strongly that these are the rules for living life.

But friends remember that we make rules, break the rules, change the rules and reframe the rules. So change the rules with the change and flow with it.

I see life as a song so follow the rhythm of music and flow with it and sing your song with the flow of music by changing your tonality and changing your behavior and your thoughts. Express your willingness to change and choose the change you want. Flow from old to new with ease and joy.

You can change yourself by doing something new, you never did before. You can flow with the flow by focusing on the new task which you choose to do to change yourself. This process will give you happiness and also change your attitude.

Always remember, first be aware of change you want to bring and then know and eliminate the hindrance or weakness which resist you to bring change. This process will make very easy for you to bring change in you.

You can not change your future, but you can change your habits, your belief systems. And sure they will change your future.

If we resist change, we fail. If we accept change, we survive. If we create change, we succeed. People sometimes do not resist change but many people do not adopt and implement change.

29) Always keep yourself Motivated

If you do not win it does not mean you lose.

Life is like an elevator and it will have series of ups and downs.

So never feel demotivated at any point of time. Even motivation is also not constant or permanent. It also comes and goes. Hence whenever you feel demotivated, take a pause and slow down. Divert your mind and thoughts to some other work or activities. Revisit your goal, rework your actions, analyze your plans, ask for help, go to your mentor and most importantly try to find the solution from within yourself. So motivate yourself. Self motivation is the best motivation.

In our life there are three feelings which always keep us motivated. These are- Abundance, Positivity and Happiness. Similarly opposite to these there are three feelings which demotivate us. These are- Scarcity, Negativity and Sorrow. If we make the habit of overcoming the feelings which demotivate us and enjoy the feelings which motivate us, then nobody can stop us from being remaining motivated all the time.

Keep away from people who try to belittle your ambitions or try to demotivate you. People often say motivation does not last forever. Well even perfume smell also does not last long. That is why you have to motivate yourself daily and regularly just like taking bath every day.

Motivation is what gets you started. Habit is what keeps you going. Attitude decides your pace and values decide your destination.

30) Express your Love, Respect and Courtesy

The love we have not given, the respect we have not shared is a waste in life. Express your love and likings to the people who are in your age group. Give respect and sympathy to your elders. Shoe courtesy and kindness to your fellow workers, staff and people below your rank. All these will create a lot of bonding in your relation. Whenever you make anyone smile you get more joy than what he gets and your heart will feel more peace. Be known as a person who care, concerns and help others when needed. Try to become a dependable person. Become a star that shines brightly by expressing your love, respect and courtesy. Be innovative and creative while expressing your love, respect, courtesy and appreciation for your loved ones and elders. Try something new so that they feel important and special.

You will find more happiness when you are able to make someone smile with your love, respect and care. Each day try to give joy, smile and happiness to anyone by doing something small. Without loving and caring heart even the richest person is a beggar of love. Spread your loving and caring net like a spider and catch in all persons that come in contact with you and sprinkle your fragrance on them to get more happiness in your life and that also without money. Even after 16 years of happy and successful marriage, every morning I wake up and wish to my wife: "Jai Shree Krishna and Love You".

People are made to be loved and things are made to be used. The confusion and problem arises in the world because people are being used and things are being loved. Always give words of encouragement when anybody fails, express your love when anybody is crying, show respect to elders and extend courtesy to seniors. Praise loudly. Showing love, respect and courtesy and having patience and politeness is not a person's weakness. It is reflection of a person's inner strength. All these qualities cost nothing but buys everything.

31) Smile and Laugh as much as in a Day

A kid knows only two things – to laugh and to cry and we all love them. Why not we adults do same thing with a little difference. To laugh and smile and make an effort to stop others crying.

Let us understand the value of a smile.
A smile costs nothing but creates much,
It enriches those who receive,
It happens in a flash but the sweet memory lasts long,
It creates happiness in home,
It fosters goodwill in business and promotes friends,
It is a rest to a tired human,
It is a daylight to discouraged and sunshine to sad,
It is a vitamin to health,
It is needed to those who have none left to give it,

So let us develop in us to SMILE whenever needed, because smile does wonders and miracles.

Now let us see the physical and scientific benefits of smile and laugh apart from emotional benefits as above.

Smile diffuses tension. Laughing secretes many chemicals in our body and put us in joyous state. Laughter brings balance in our body. Laughter therapy is used to treat many ailments and irregularity in our body. A smile is the lighting system of face, cooling system of heart, sparkling system of eyes and relaxing system of mind!

It is not necessary that you should laugh when you are happy but in order to keep yourself happy you should laugh. Laughter is the shortest distance between two people.

A day without laughter is a day wasted. Humor is by far the most significant activity of the human brain.

Smiles and silence are two powerful tools. A smile is the way to solve many problems and silence is the way to avoid many problems.

A man or woman is fully and well dressed only if he or she carries a smile.

32) Stick to your Duties and not results

It is said that count on your efforts but never count on your results. You have to stick to your duties and act and the result is bound to follow.

First make up your mind what to start and what not to start and then complete what you start. Success never goes to those who start and left unfinished. Success always goes to those who start and finishes in spite of all adverse circumstances and situations. In fact the difference between the success and failure is nothing but to start and finish.

Perform your duties with the talent and skills you have and give 100% of yours to it. You do not need to be perfect in all your talents and skills but whatever you give that should be 100% perfect of yours and the result is bound to follow.

If only the best bird sang, the forest would be silent.

First put your efforts and labor and perform your duties with heart and soul and the result ought to come. It is the byproduct and/or joint product of your duties. It may be money, satisfaction or recognition. It is the Universal Law of Nature that gives you result. The result may not be sometimes up to your expectation or it may be delayed but never give up your duties. The Nature keeps record of all your duties and efforts and it will give result at proper time and in manifold.

If you know you are doing the right things, just relax and perform. Forget about outcome. You can not control anything anyway

33) Never find Faults but Overlook it

No one is perfect in this world. Everyone has their own flaws and weakness. If you search for flaws you will surely discover but that is not our greatness. Our greatness lies in appreciating the good qualities, strength and helping others in overcoming their flaws and weakness. Our maturity lies in ignoring petty flaws and weakness of others. This is particularly hold good with our family members, friends, relatives and colleagues. If you continuously find flaws and weakness of such people, it will not only make them sad but you will also be sad as these people will try to stay away from you and may dislike you. So with broader mind and open heart accept these people as they are and always appreciate them for their good qualities and strengths and learn from that. Never pin point their fault and weakness. When they realize themselves about their flaws and weakness, help them to correct it.

Never carry BMW brand with you, means never known as Blamers, Markers and Whiners.

A wise man is one who forgets the faults of others, but always remembers his own. You are great if you can find your faults. You are

greater if you can remove/reduce your faults. You are greatest if you accept and love others with their faults. It is like buy and accept on "as is where is basis".

When a man points a finger at someone else to find faults, he should remember that three of his fingers are pointing at himself.

34) Your Permission is required to Hurt or Insult You

Whenever you feel unhappy or sad, just listen to your heart and place your hand on your heart and ask – What type of your thoughts in which your mind is indulging and what emotions your heart is carrying and you will find your cause of unhappiness or sad. Very often you will see that it is only you who is making you sad by your emotions and thoughts.

Life is 90% how we take situations and stock memory in our mind and 10% is how we respond to it.

So whenever you have negative feelings when someone hurt or insult you, take the experience as an experiment for your development and to make you stronger mentally.

Suppose you got injury, burn or wound on any part of your body then what would you do? You will apply ointment and will bandage it. Then slowly and gradually it gets healed. So is the case with hurt or insult. Although time is the best medicine to forget it. But even then you have to take your own course of action to do away with it as early as possible.

If we understand the fact that people are not difficult but they are different in their attitude and behavior we can build great relationships and avoid many sour relationships and get rid of getting hurt by people. No one can make you feel inferior without your consent.

35) Make a mission for your life

The future is in our hands. We make our own fortune. So make a mission for your life and march for it year on year, month on month, day on day, minute to minute and second to second. The great thing in the world is not where we stand but in what direction we are moving in pursuance of a mission.

To make a mission for your life, enlighten your thinking. Those who really seek the path to enlightenment, dictate terms to their mind. Then they proceed with strong determination. Mission for life means you have to set certain principles which clearly states where you want to go or what you want to achieve in your life. It is the final destination you want to reach before the end of your life. Mission statement describes your value. It is like head light of a car which always shows the way. It keeps you focused all the time and governs your life. It is also necessary to analyze and review your mission statement whenever you feel so. You can quickly redirect your efforts and thoughts if someone tries to get you off track from your mission. Print mission of your life on your visiting cards, letter heads and make a poster of it and hang it in your office chamber and on the wall of your bedroom.

Every man has a right to choose his own destiny.

Success in life depends upon two important things:

1) Vision: Seeing the invisible
2) Mission: doing the impossible.

36) Be Kind and show Gratitude like a Flower

Implement Principle and follow Discipline like an Iron

Always behave yourself in a polite, soft and courteous manner. To get respect you must first give respect.

Similarly implement principle and follow discipline as strong as iron. This will help you to get success in achieving your goal and make your life disciplined.

It is very important to strike a balance between your soft approach and strong attitude. If you are able to balance the two successfully your life will be happy and full of joy.

Always make yourself a better friend by showing your kindness and a good citizen by following strictly disciplines and principles of life.

Never play with the feelings of people. You may win the moment but the risk is that you will surely lose the person. Be known as someone with cool head, warm heart and great character.

It is better to lose your ego to the one you love than to lose the one you love because of ego. If you desire to blossom like a rose in the garden, you have to learn the art of adjusting with the thorns.

If you can not be a pencil to write anyone's happiness, try at least to be a nice eraser to erase everyone's sorrows!

People who value their privileges above their principles and disciplines soon lose both. This is so because excuses are the easiest things to manufacture and the hardest things to sell.

37) Remove Phobia of Public Speaking

It takes courage to walk your talk.

Every man thinks and express his thoughts but very few people spread it. This is so because they scare to go to masses. Many people have the phobia of speaking on mike over stage and to spread and express his thoughts in public.

So remove the phobia and make it is one of your goal to speak in public on mike over stage freely whenever you get opportunity or chance. Mastering the art of public speaking takes you to a greater height. You will get extra mileage and an edge over others by this communication skill.

Plan what to say, how to say, how to listen, how to express yourself. Moreover in communication, pause also plays a vital role. So take pause while answering any question. Moreover you should ensure and confirm that your message has been conveyed rightly without any deletion and distortion.

Two things indicate our weakness: To be silent when it is proper to speak! And to speak when it is proper to be silent.

38) Appreciate and Love Yourself

Learn to appreciate yourself. You are not bad just because someone else is better.

Everyone suffers from self hatred and guilt so make yourself happy by appreciating yourself even for the smallest of the smallest good deed or achievement. "I am not capable". "I am not Good", "I am a Failure" etc etc never make such statement to yourself and never make it a bottom line excuse in your life.

We must learn to love ourselves. Self approval and self acceptance is most necessary to bring positive change within yourself. Life becomes very smooth when we love and appreciate ourselves.

Speak loudly and tell yourself the following at least once in a day:

I am living in a perfect, whole and complete Universe with infinite resources. The God always guides and protects me. I am living in the present and by looking within myself I expand my future. I rise above my problems. I love myself and all is well in my world.

Also support yourself when you feel no one is with you. Reward and recognize yourself even for the smallest of your achievement. By doing this your mind, body and spirit gets new energy. You will move to the next level of peak performance.

The secret of Happiness is the acceptance of yourself.

39) Life is an Adventure, Dare it

There are certain thrilling activities which many people never dare to do it. These activities include- swimming, water rafting, scuba diving, rock climbing, trekking, parasailing, camping, sky diving, ski, skating, desert safari, jungle safari, fire fighting etc etc. Do at least one or two activities which you are scared and enjoy it. Learn it and train yourself if necessary before doing it. But do it in your life. This will bring out child within you. This will give liveliness to your life. Your spirit will revitalize. It will keep your zeal active and you will feel younger.

I have done scuba diving, parasailing, desert safari and jungle safari.

I have made my goal to do sky diving in New Zealand by 31st March, 2015

40) Retire Right

To retire right, I mean to retire at right age (a little early if possible) from your career job/business, making yourself free from all such duties and responsibilities and redirecting your effort and thought towards some noble cause of contribution to society and of course with enough money to take care of your balance estimated life span. Try not to be dependent on your next generation both physically and financially. If possible also stay alone and separately from your next generation and let them live their own life. This does not mean that you do not care for them or they do not care for them, also this does not mean that both of you do not love and care each other. I mean you can have freedom in your life if you do so. I believe that in every relationship there should be freedom to all and for all. By giving freedom and space in every relationship, it grows and develops of its own and to the fullest.

C) CAREER AND FINANCIAL MANAGEMENT

41) Focus on your goal

Everything is created twice in the earth. First it comes into existence within undefined and unvested imaginary boundaries of your mind and then into reality. There are six steps to remain focused on your goal are:

1. Think it
2. Ink it
3. Believe it
4. Visualize it
5. Feel it
6. Ready to receive it

There are three benefits of remaining focused on your goal are:

1. Goals says what you want in life and help you to focus only on those activities to achieve your goal
2. Focusing on goals helps you to identify opportunities and seek new opportunities
3. Focusing on goals decides your course of actions, sets your priorities and motivates you to achieve goals. Something magical happens when you write down your goals, remain focused on goals related to all spheres of life –physical, mental, career, professional, social and spiritual.

Your life is determined by your dominant desire. You can prepare slogan based on your goal and aim in life and print it on your letter head and visiting cards. Goal should scare you a little but excite a lot. By recording your dreams and goals on paper, you set in motion the process of becoming the person you want to be. Whatever the mind can conceive and believe, it can achieve. People with goals succeed because they know where they are going.

42) Make Small List of SMART Goals

Too many hands spoils the cooking. Similarly too many goals in life makes life miserable. I would say too many goals means no goal. This is so because if you have too many goals and tries to achieve all the goals at a time, you will be lost and you might have to make emergency landing over sea. I would advise you to break your goals into 4 categories:

1. Physical and Health
2. Social and Emotional
3. Career and Finance
4. Spiritual and Humanity.

Divide each category into 3 sub categories- Short Term (1month to 1 year), Medium Term (1 year to 5 year) and Long Term (up to 10 year). Set 2 goals for each sub category, that means you are setting 6 goals for each category and total 24 goals.

This means you are trying to achieve 8 goals within 12 months, 8 goals within 60 months and 8 goals within 120 months. In other words you are trying to achieve 24 goals in 120 months. Don't you think you can give enough time to achieve all these goals from whatever perspective you think??

Review and replace the goals at the end of each year as the case may be. And yes set SMART goals. SMART means- Specific, Measurable, Achievable, Realistic and Time Bound. So set your goals as per your priority

A person with a clear purpose will make progress on even the roughest road. A person with no purpose will make no progress on even the smoothest road.

43) Plan and Work Smartly to achieve your Goal

Just be better than the average and keep going. It is the way to reach the pinnacle.

Winners never quit, they simply adjust before taking next step.

Develop the winning edge, small differences in your performance can lead to large differences in your results.

All of the above are some of the ways of working smartly.

Similarly planning is also of equal importance to achieve goal. This is so because good goal is just converted into wish without good planning. Let us visualize a situation with Goal, Plan and Work (GPW). Imagine a two storied building as your house as your goal at a certain place by a certain date. Make a mental road map as our mobile does with GPRS to reach that house (Goal). This mental road map is your plan to achieve the goal. Then start your body machine and run on the road (with Plan) to reach the house. You work with your body machine in which sometimes you have to work hard and sometimes work with intelligence and do smart work. This is how goal is achieved. Remember there is no short cut. Execute your plan as early as possible and never hold your plan just like holding file in government offices. Also review your plan and analyze your work regularly to rectify mistakes.

We are focused so much on today's problems that we put off planning for tomorrow's opportunities. Lack of confidence born out of lack of planning.

Great things are not done by impulse, but by a series of planning small things brought together.

44) Have Faith and Keep Patience to Achieve Goal and Believe in Yourself

Take yourself seriously. Never think what people will say about you and why they will laugh at you. This is so because common people laugh at when they do not understand you, reject you if they are not able to adjust or adopt to your thoughts. Never have the fear of laughter of the crowd. Just forget and never care what people think. What is more important is to think about yourself, to have faith in yourself to achieve goal and to believe in yourself and your goal.

If you have tried and failed in achieving your goal, then never let it down but keep your patience and wait for good time because time is the perfect healer of mistakes, failures and grievances. There will come a time which will turn the whole fate and bring you success to achieve your goal. Patience is a bitter plant but it has a sweet fruit.

Self confidence and believe in yourself are of utmost importance to achieve goal.

The best measure of the belief in yourself is your persistence. Your courage to be persistent in spite of adverse situation and circumstances and your ability and capability to bounce back and start a fresh after temporary setback will give you success.

There are no limits to what you can accomplish except for the limits you place on your imagination. And since there is no limits to what you can imagine, there are no limits to what you can achieve.

The only thing that stands between a man and his goals of life is what merely the will to try and the faith to believe that it is possible. Every achiever that I have heard. said one thing in common that. "My life turned around when I began to believe in me".

Your chances of success in any anything can always be measured by your belief in yourself. People become really remarkable when they start thinking that they can do things. When they believe in themselves, they have the first secret of success.

45) Always take harder way to achieve your goal

There may be short cuts, there may be easier ways, there may be more explored, tried and tested way but to get the real taste of your success, achievement and pleasure to enjoy the fruits of your goal and to make a lasting impression not only for you, but for the mankind as a whole, always choose harder way, longer way and less travelled way or you can explore your way also to achieve goal and success.

This is based on the simple rule- No Risk No gain, Moderate Risk Moderate Gain, Higher Risk Higher Gain. Can anyone plan for everything?? In life there may come a situation with lot of uncertainty and for which you cannot plan but even then you have to take action. You have to show courage to choose one path. Here courage means you have the knowledge of risk but you have to take risk to achieve something. Always remember risk itself get mitigated once you ready to face it and start taking actions.

There are no short cuts to any place worth going. To achieve any significant goal you must leave your comfort zone. We have either physical comfort zones or we develop mental, emotional, social or psychological comfort zones.

Ships are safest in the harbor but they are not meant to be there. They have to sail long, hard and face stormy seas to reach the comfort of a desirable destination.

46) Concentrate on your work

Doing work or study with full concentration is of great importance. Concentration means giving 100% of your physical and mental attention and involvement for the work or study you do. Concentration brings perfection and accuracy. It adds value to your work. To concentrate you should have clear mind and silence if possible. Breathing techniques help mind to concentrate. If you do what you love than concentration will come automatically.

To get manifold concentration on work delicate it to your subordinate with full power and authority and he will not disappoint you either sometimes they will do better than you.

The quickest way to do so many things is to do only one thing at a time. Our success will be largely determined by our ability to concentrate single mindedly on one thing at a time. The person who tries to do everything, accomplishes nothing.

Concentrate all your thoughts upon the work at hand. The sun's rays do not burn until brought to a focus.

47) Master your time, Master your life

Time is the most precious and valuable thing in the world. God has given 24 hours to all. but it is up to us how to use it or waste it. It is said "time and tide waits for none "so if one is able to manage time will be able to manage his life very easily. If you are the master of your time then you are the master of your life. At the end of each day ask yourself how I spent my time and energy for the day. Feel satisfaction and proud by completing your work before time. It is well said that time is money. Time earned and invested in right manner helps you to become rich in all ways.

Time Management Technique:

Break your day from the moment you wake up into 30 minute slot till you go to bed. Note down activities you did in every 30 minute slot. Classify your activities into 4 categories. A- Must Do activities related to your physical and mental, social and emotional, spiritual and humanity, B- Must Do activities related to your Career and Finance, C- can be avoided activities and D- Must Avoid activities. So, snatch time from D- Must Avoid Activities and steal some time from C- Can Be Avoided activities and use that saved time for some other activities as per your priority. Use your transportation and travel time. While walking you can think and plan your schedule and activities, you can practice within any speech which you are suppose to deliver.

If you travel in a chauffeur driven car, hear some motivational audio CD or read newspaper. If you are travelling, the best use of time you can make is to read a book or even you can write a book. I would suggest always carry a book and your personal journal with you. If you are fond of reading or writing then start reading or writing whenever you get chance. You control your life by controlling your time.

Until we manage time, we are capable of managing anything. Do not say that you do not have enough time. God has given equal 24 hours or 86400 seconds to every man in this world. When time never stops for us, then why do we always wait for time. All time is right time.

48) Make first impression

It is said that the first impression is the last impression. So make your first impression as the lasting impression

Today's age is the age of value addition So do value addition to your life by making an impression, the more you add value to your life more money you will make

The value addition can be done in any of the following ways to make first impression:

1. To speak something new which no one knows but everyone likes
2. To dress uniquely to be liked by majority to impress more person
3. To behave in a very friendly and polite way so that everyone loves to be with you
4. To do or act something differently that everyone likes/loves you with impressing personality.
5. To show sympathy and generosity to create impression.

Your First Impression should be MERCEDES means- Motivated, Energetic, Resourceful, Committed, Educated, Dedicated, Enterprising and Smart.

One of the adverse impact in making first impression is that stupid ones pretend that they know everything whereas intelligent ones doubt everything.

49) Listen more, speak less

To listen actively, carefully and with attention is an art. It is the art more difficult to practice than to practice the art of speaking. By listening you are giving respect to the speaker. You can learn while listening. Speak only when you are asked to speak and ask the right question. Remember never interrupt the speaker and never speak on behalf of speaker by completing his sentences. Silence or keeping quiet and listening patiently gives you strength and knowledge.

Speaking to the point and precise is a sign of strong mind and clear thought. Kind words can be short and easy to speak, but their effect is truly enormous. A learned man knows- learning comes from listening, not talking alone. There are essentially two things that will make us wiser: the more we listen and less we speak. The funny part of communication: We listen half, understand quarter and speak double. Make sure you have finished speaking before the audience stops you listening. 90% of the life's problems are due to the tone of voice; it is not what we say, it is how we say it that creates problems. Do not raise your voice, improve quality of your discussions. Remember you can recover from injury caused by slip of foot but you may not make up the damage caused by slip of tongue. The right word spoken at the right time sometimes achieves miracles. A speech without a specific purpose is like a journey without a destination. Our speaking is well shaped and sharpened by our reading as well as our listening. Knowledge speaks but wisdom listens. Mere silence is not wisdom. For wisdom consists of knowing when and how to speak, what to speak and when to speak. The most valuable of all talents is that of never using two words when one will do. Hard words cannot touch any soft heart, but soft words can touch any hard heart. God has given us two ears and one tongue for a reason- to listen twice and then to speak. When you are speaking, you are only repeating what you already know. But if you listen, you may learn something new.

50) Be disciplined, be punctual

Discipline and punctuality are very vital qualities of highly successful person. It reflects the character of a person and it gives respect and regards to other. Never be too early and never be to late being on time is being effective.

Always treat your job as a sacred trust. Do it religiously, in a strict disciplined manner and keep your commitment and be dependable. This will not only motivate others but will help you to achieve greater and greater accomplishment. People count disciplined person.

The disciplined person just follow the discipline, rules and regulations.

Life never grows great until it is focused, dedicated, disciplined, punctual and committed. Success is nothing more than a few simple disciplines practiced daily and failure is nothing more than a few small errors repeated daily.

A wise and great man shows his wisdom and greatness by being on time 90%. In reading the lives of great men, I found that the self victory they won was over themselves. Self discipline with all of them came first.

The price of discipline is always less than the pain of regret. Much of the stress that people feel does not come from having too much to do. It comes from not finishing in time what they started late.

51) Plan and schedule your day, week, month, year

Schedule your day with work to do and appointments to be kept

Plan your week before the week starts for the very short term goal and targets and to finish the unfinished work of last week

Plan your next month for the short term goals and for the commitment to be fulfilled

Plan your year ahead for the long term and big goals

Never feel that you are over worked for your day, week, month or year.

Monday is a tough day for many, yet it brings lot of optimism for the coming week. Always feel Monday Blues.

Similarly give importance to 1st day of the month for setting your monthly targets and 1st day of the year for setting your yearly and long term goals.

Life is to move forward with every second. Plan your day, week, month, year and so on with a purpose. Write down one-two big and important task you want to complete today, 2-3 task for the week, 3-5 task for the month, 5-10 task for the year. Make those task as your priority. Always remember to choose big task first as Big Rocks First.

A good plan of today is better than a great plan tomorrow. Do not judge each day by the harvest you reap but by the seeds that you plant.

52) Take Baby Step and Start Small

By this I mean you should start something new of your own. In other words, you should take initiative to do something without being told to do so. Taking initiative is a challenge and make it an habit, it will lead to accept greater responsibility and greater responsibility brings greater achievements. Small beginnings make large endings.

Every ambitious and potential man start a small business of their own because he always looks forward and do planning to do big. Remember baby steps end up in running and you may cross a benchmark and set a new milestone. You must dream big when working on it, to achieve that big, break it into small parts and then start achieving small targets, very soon you will see your big dream is coming closer to you. The journey of a thousand miles begins with a single step.

Let us take example: If you are Life Insurance agent and want to collect Rs. 2 core of premium in a year. This is a big dream because it will make you Top of the Million Dollar Round Table. So break it into small premium of 50000 to 1 lac and try to sell policy daily with such premium. How sound this and good to collect small premium of 50000-1 lac daily and you may see that your goal of 2crore is achieved before the end of the year.

Knowing is not enough; we must apply. Willing is not enough; we must act. Become a man of deed not man of words.

The world is not a parking lot, it is a racing track. Keep on moving. Take first step in faith. You do not have to see the whole staircase. Just take the first step. An idea that is developed and put into action is more important than an idea that exists only as an idea. It is not the 'deficiency of knowledge' but the 'efficiency of execution' that separates achievers from the losers. If you really want to start something' you will find a way, else you will always find excuse. By doing and starting you will understand.

53) Build your Own Success and Motivational Mantra

The successful person has the habit of doing things which failures do not like to do. Failures do not like doing them either necessarily. But their disliking is subordinated to the strength of their purpose. The success has its own definition and meaning. For some people success is accumulation of wealth, for some it is rendering great service to mankind, for some it is to earn name, fame and status, for some it is to become good parents, for some it is adventure also. So build your own success mantra and stick to it, plan to achieve it and motivate yourself all the time till you achieve it. Never become servant of your thoughts but make your thought servant of your will. You are master of your own mind. If you think of success and you will be successful.

Make your own slogan or tag line and say to yourself as many times in a day to give energy to your body and strengthen your soul. If you have the will to win, you have achieved half of your success; if you do not have, you have achieved half of your failure.

54) Work Hard and Smart

You can never achieve anything without hard labor, exercising of best judgment and careful planning and working extra hours. You have to put your 100% mind, body, soul and spirit.

A man feels happy and relief when he has put his heart into his work, whereas a man feels unhappy and sad when he says something and does otherwise.

The color of hard work and fruits of smart work always bring success.

A sleeping lobster is carried away by the water current.

It is said that if you work 8 hours a day, you are working for survival. If you work for 10 hours a day, you get success. If you work for 12 hours a day, then success becomes your habit and you are successful and taken as veteran in your business/profession.

There is no alternative to hard work and there is no short cut to hard work.

Hard work also includes smart work. One way of doing smart work is to do hard jobs first and the easy jobs will take care of themselves.

This means – Work hard Specific Work

Work Hard with Magnitude of Work.

Work Hard All time

Work Hard till Result comes

Work Hard with Time Binding.

I am a great believer inluck, and I find the harder I work the more I have of it. For me LUCK means Labour Under Complete Knowledge. Hard work is like a staircase and luck is like a lift. The lift may fail but, the staircase is sure to take you to the top. Success is 10% inspiration and 90% is perspiration. It is true that every effort and hard work is not converted into success, but it is equally true that success does not come without effort and hard work.

Everything is easy when you are busy in your workings! But nothing is easy when you are lazy.

55) Take Opinion of Three People Before Taking Decision

There are three types of friends- one who motivate you, second show you the darker side and third always remains with you. Others are not friends.

So always take advice of three such people. A person who want to march ahead requires 3 people- One who leads him, second who march with him and third who is at the back of him.

The first one is our leader, mentor, guru and motivates us to march ahead and leads us by example. The second one always remains with you in good days or in bad days. The third one takes care of everything at the back of you. So always follow these three persons and take their advice.

Find such 3 persons and meet them regularly to take feedback from them. Give them patient and attentive listening and discuss and make logical arguments with them. Take a note of their wise advice and counsel and make out a strategy.

Believing and following everybody is dangerous but believing and following nobody is very dangerous and very risky also. Follow HALT method of making successful decision. This means never take decision when you are Hungry, Angry, Lonely or Tired.

56) Build a Supportive and Cooperative Team

Teamwork can achieve so much more. Ever since I have realized this, I do not want to do anything alone. It is hard to achieve something alone. The man who has the ability and good judgment to get his work done through others is chosen as a leader and not the person who does his work with his own hands. So if you want to grow in your life upwards you have to build a supportive and cooperative team under you. Moreover, it is also your duty when you move to a higher level to teach the incoming leader how to handle his team, explaining him strength and weakness of the team.

A happy and successful leader usually disposes the work by delegating to different heads and manages and controls, supervises and motivate those heads.

A good team rocks. It strengthens the capacity to perform extraordinary. Believe in yourself and the people around you.

A supportive and cooperative team brings the power of unity. It is very exciting and it creates bonding in relationship to march towards goal with everyone together.

Now-a-days you can even build online support team or network.

Talent wins games but teamwork and intelligence win championships. If we did all the things we are capable of, we would literally astound ourselves.

57) Be Passionate not Possessive

If you have passion for what you are doing, you are going to do it much harder. The more you are passionate about your work, the more chances are likely to succeed. If your job is what you love to do, you will surely have passion for your job. When psychologist Vera John Steiner interviewed one hundred creative people, she found they all had one thing in common, an intense passion for their work.

Be Passionate, not Possessive. Being passionate sets you free. Being possessive holds you back. Never do things/job just for money, it will never bring you success, but if you love what you are doing then it will give you satisfaction and success also.

Similarly, be passionate about money but not possessive. This is so because possessing money will never give you happiness but earning and enjoying with money will give you happiness. Money will buy you a house but not a home; a bed but not a sound night sleep; a companion but not a friend; a good time but not a peace of mind

Life takes "passion, determination and skill." You can not skip any of these three and expect to enjoy success built to last.

Only passion, firm determination and excellent skills can elevate the life.

58) Follow Ten Commandments to increase our Business

To increase and grow your business follow the following 10 Principles:

1. Always add at least 10% new names in the list of your clients/customers.
2. Try to retain at least 95% of your existing clients/customers.
3. Increase your turnover by at least 10% in terms of monetary value
4. Sell at least 10% more to your existing clients in terms of monetary value
5. Sell at least 10% more to your existing clients in terms of volume say no of orders or no of units.
6. Build a sales team and strong networking force
7. Sell by telling stories.
8. Get testimonials from your valued and satisfied clients/customers and use it as advertisement/publicity.
9. Build rapport and personal relation with your clients/customers to make strong bonding
10. Take even smallest complain of your customer/client seriously and correct it

59) Analyze and make a note of your day

If your life is worth for you, make it more worthy by writing about it. At the end of each day analyze how was your day. Whatever you did in the entire day, divide it into 5 categories. There are:

1. Time spent on your physical and mental activities
2. Time spent on your career and finance activities
3. Time spent on your social and emotional activities
4. Time spent on your spiritual activities
5. Time wasted is time spent not on any of the above four activities

Try to minimize your usage of time in 5 of the categories. Plan your next days schedule just before sleeping the previous day.

Thank god for his kindness for giving us another day to live with full potential

Make a habit of sitting quietly before going to bed and note down two most good thing happened and two worst thing happened. This will help you in overcoming your mistakes and shortcoming. Never think that a day with 24 hours went wrong or not enough for you.

To write your daily experiences along with the results and lessons you received from it will act as a catalyst to make you more wiser and will give new dimension to your life. To make a note of your day is your one-to-one meeting and conversation with yourself.

60) Be positive and increase positivity

If you are positive and hopeful, you will attract positive and good thing and positive thing will happen in your life and you will feel happy

You can increase positivity in your life by speaking loudly a same positive thought everyday or by writing it every day. The idea is really helpful for maintaining top performance.

If you want to develop any positivity in the form of positive feeling, positive attitude, positive mind frame, positive thoughts, positive speaking or positive viewing, you can develop it by following the Rule of 21. The rule says that if you do and practice it religiously, consecutively, with your body, heart and soul, at a fixed time, with a fixed mindset and belief then it becomes your habit. The habit will be installed in your sub consciousness mind. It is said that we first make our habits and then our habits make us. The human body and mind frame is nothing but skeleton of our habits. So build positive habits to increase positivity. This is so because only positivity will make your progress and protects you from holding back. So make yourself an Empire with Powerful King and Soldiers in the form of positive habits and attitude.

When you think positive, it happens! When you think negative, it happens too! We must finite disappointment but must believe in infinite hope.

61) Conserve and Enrich your Reputation

Reputation is the most precious treasure you possess. A person with good reputation can scale new peaks in life. Reputation is like hard disk of a computer. If it crashes then we lose valuable data. Similarly reputation once gone it is very difficult to retrieve your character, identity and integrity. So never do anything for which we feel shame in telling to our family or friends or society. No matter how hard you pretend, others will notice this at some point of time. It will whitewash your lifelong reputation at a stroke. Be genuine, Be Natural, Be Honest and Be yourself.

To build a good reputation one should be careful in using the words when one speaks because words spoken lightly and casually may not be kept. In other words, promises and words given will be broken. When we fail to keep our promise or word, we lose credibility. When we lose credibility we lose faith and when faith is lost our reputation goes. I understand that in today's world it is very difficult to abide 100% by our words and promises. So be careful in making promises or commitment and be tactful also. By tactful I mean keep yourself open while making promise or commitment so that even if you fail to keep your word, you have the way to explain or clarify yourself genuinely the cause of your failure so that your reputation is not at stake.

The difference between ability and reputation is that ability will get you on the top and character will keep you there. Character cannot be developed easily and rapidly. By experiencing happiness and sorrow, soul gets purified, ambition inspired, success achieved and reputation can be gained.

If we have integrity and reputation, nothing else matters. If we do not have integrity and reputation, nothing else matters.

Surround yourself with reputed people. You will be the average of the five reputed people you spend the time with him.

62) Find a Life Mentor

We all need someone to believe in us and to encourage us. Attend, lectures, seminars, watch videos and DVDs, read books written by your favorite author and listen Audio CDs. Always take spending on all these as your investment. Also consult your mentor and take lessons and coaching from him regularly or whenever you need. This is so because you can learn some powerful methods and techniques out of these and you can earn in multiples when you implement such methods and techniques. Always remember by reading a book you are reading a person with several years of experience and by attending lectures or watching DVD, you are watching a person live or in action with practice of several hours. Also invest your time with your life mentor.

You can have more than one mentor. Make a list of your mentors or ideals whom you want to follow in your life or want to become like that. Also list down the qualities which you like in them and you want to adopt in your life. Mention achievements of those ideals by the side of their name which you also want to make goal of your life. Let me explain you by my example. Indian Cricketer Sunil Gavaskar is one of my ideals. I liked his quality that he used to face all fast bowlers of his time without wearing helmet on his head. Moreover he has scored most of his runs and hit maximum centuries against fast bowlers of West Indies. In his time even the other great batsman fear the fury of West Indian fast bowlers and seldom dare to face them without helmet. So I have noted this quality and decided that I will face every difficult situation in my life single handedly and will try my utmost best to overcome it.

The man who does not read good books has no advantage over the man who can not read it. This is so because readers are leaders and leaders are readers. That is why it is sais said that reading is to the mind what exercise is to the body.

63) There is no Power in Knowledge but Knowledge is Powerful

The gates of knowledge and learning are always open, and open for all. You will find many people who are not much learned or scholar but achieved great success in their life. Dhirubhai Ambani is one such person and my Ideal. Then what makes them so successful. It is their burning desire to achieve something and their thirst to acquire knowledge and ideas and put them into practice.

I compare knowledge with knife. If knife is blunt it cannot cut even a piece of paper. But if it is sharpened then it can cut even wood or iron. Similarly if you acquire entire world' knowledge but do not use and apply it then you are like a blunt knife. On the other hand, whatever knowledge you acquire and put them into use then it can make you powerful.

The more you gather knowledge, the more you apply, the more you achieve and the more you achieve, the more powerful you become.

So knowledge not used is a garbage. People respect you not for the knowledge you have, but the way you utilize it.

I practice and follow Dhirubhai Ambani as my Role Model. I would strongly recommend to read his biography.

An investment in knowledge always pays the best interest. A man of wealth has many enemies, while a man of knowledge has many friends.

Knowledge becomes obsolete every few years. If you do not renew your knowledge often and thoroughly you can become obsolete and fall behind.

You should be greedy about acquiring knowledge and impatient to apply knowledge.

64) Ignite your Will Power and Confidence

Win yourself not others.

If you do what you say, one day the world will start doing what you say.

Believe in your own ability and capability to do big things. You can compel others to have faith in you, only if you have more than 100% faith and confidence in yourself.

One way of building self confidence is to do better and better each day and each time what we are doing regularly. You should be able to produce better result with less utilization of resources both mental and physical.

Make yourself an iron man with strong will power and demand much from yourself and also be your hardest trainer. Never feel low about yourself and never value yourself down.

A person with strong will power and confidence will not fall back against any situation or circumstances.

> You can do some weight lifting. This will make you mentally strong and tough. It is believed that physically strong people (not fatty people) are mentally tough people but very kind at heart. They have strong will power and confidence but soft speaking.

If you do not have courage, confidence and will power, you may not have an opportunity to use any of your other virtues.

65) Increase your Capacity and Potential

Human muscle is like spring. If we stretch it and stretch it, it will expand and on release it will regain its original position. Similarly we can increase our capacity by pushing ourselves little harder and little farther each day. By doing this our capacity will increase. If we can increase our capacity then our output and potential to generate more output will increase. If a factory runs at optimum capacity producing maximum output will generate more sales and achieves higher profit.

One very important and less explored way of communication to increase your capacity and potential is TO ASK. Whenever you are in any forum, seminar, conference, or public meeting and you do not understand any point of speaker, feel free to ask. You will not only be highlighted but you will get focused and personalized reply from the speaker which give you learning and knowledge and will increase your capacity and potential. Never feel shame or scare from asking anywhere. A Chinese proverb says: "He who asks may be a fool for five minutes but who does not ask is a fool for a lifetime." A person has the chance of getting what he wants if he asks for that but a person who does not ask may not have even chance of getting it.

A man is not paid for having a head and hands but for using them. We judge ourselves by what we feel capable of doing, while others judge us by what we have already done.

Do not decrease your goal to the extent of your ability, increase your ability to the extent of your goal. The difference between a successful person and others is not lack of strength, not lack of knowledge, but rather lack of will power.

When you settle for mediocrity in the small goals; you will also begin to settle for mediocrity in the big goals. The more we study, the more we discover our ignorance and the more will be our capacity.

Most people overestimate their problems and underestimate their potential.

66) Create Lively Work Environment and System and work with Enthusiasm

Work environment and systems and equipments in the organization should create lively environment for all working people and they should be able to work efficiently. It should help people to work smoothly, efficiently and work intelligently by combining their efforts jointly as a team to achieve best result. They should work with enthusiasm. The best sign of showing enthusiasm in any work is ability and willingness to assume higher responsibility. Change your attitude towards your office mate and your subordinate and spare some time and give some effort to help them.

The environment should be such that laborious job does not feel tiring and painful and paper work job not boring. Create a system for everything. Now-a-days technology has so advanced that you can track your staff the moment he enters the office till he leave the office for the day.

Motivate those around you, work with them and work for them and they will eventually live up to the expectations. If you put them down and they have no reason to do any better.

67) Always Upgrade and Update Yourself

An apple a day keeps the doctors away. An hour of reading a day keeps the ignorance away. Always upgrade yourself by acquiring knowledge and skill required for your work and update yourself with the latest development in technology. This will increase your efficiency to work. How efficient you are in your work and how valuable are you to your organization is determined by the supervision you require.

I believe that curiosity and necessity are the mother of all invention. Every question comes with an answer like every lock has a key and all questions bring curiosity and all answers brings knowledge along with it. Always show your intention to grow by upgrading and updating yourself. Without continuous upgrading and updating no progress and growth is possible and if it is so then words like improvement, success and achievement has no meaning.

An idea can change your life so always look for ideas.

See every opportunity as chance to learn and upgrade and update yourself with the learning. This is the true sign of mature, secure and growing person. Remember even trainer takes training, teachers take teachings, coaches go for coaching themselves. Reinforce, redesign and reframe your learning.

Victory and success will come in search of us if we upgrade and update us regularly. Spend at least 10-20% of your daily work time in understanding, learning and adopting new skills and techniques to do a particular job.

I believe people should study a little bit every day. It should become habitual, like brushing your teeth, combing your hair, having a shower or getting dressed.

Knowledge becomes obsolete every few years. If you do not renew your knowledge often and thoroughly you can become obsolete and fall behind.

68) Avoid chatting, gossip

Gossiping, chatting, surfing social sites is all waste of time. Poor people talk of other people and cover up their own fault.

Rich people always think of great ideas and new ideas. Ideas get even better when you share them. Ideas can transform someone. Ideas can expand imagination.

On the other hand, chatting and gossips limits your progress and development as it attracts negativity and negative energy. People who waste time in chatting and gossiping end up with nothing.

All work gives either satisfaction or money.

All gossip brings either frustration or poverty.

The innovation in technology and communication tools- telephone, mobile, sms, emails, whatsapp, skype, etc etc are the most effective time savers but at the time also greatest tools for chatting and gossiping, so limit and restrict the use of all these gadgets for your purpose and benefits only and stay away from it.

Hard work pays off in the future and often give positive results. Laziness, chatting and gossiping gives instant and often negative results.

Conversation is an exercise of the brain. Gossip is a brainless exercise of the tongue.

69) Slow down in Unfavorable Circumstances

Take calculated risk. Slow down and take a pause when situations and circumstances are not favorable. Think over it, listen to your heart and take tips from mentor and then rework and reframe your ideas to march ahead.

Never test the depth of the river with both feet together.

Suppose a nasty driver who drives roughly wants to overtake you, then will you like to race with him or give him pass. Similarly in life when the circumstance are unfavorable and you stuck with anyone, then slow down and let the time pass and then move.

Sometimes slowing down yields better results and makes life more enjoyable. He who stops being better, stops being good.

If you find yourself in a hole, the first thing to do is stop digging. All work and no rest takes the spring and bound out of the most vigorous life. Slowing down in adverse time and resting is not time wasted but time gained.

70) Minimize use of media

Now a days we are bombarded with information from various media source like radio, T.V, emails, paper websites, magazines and surrounded by lots of gadgets like mobile, smart phones, laptops, I-pods, I-pads, tablets, video games etc.

All this keeps us busy and eat lots of our time and we are left with very less time for productive and creative work

The success of media is based on selling negative news. The media that cover the sizzling crime or the cruel tragedy is more popular than media that highlights great social acts of great human being or reports latest scientific discovery/invention

Try not to read or watch any negative news. This will help you to focus more on positive news and you will feel more motivated.

Read newspaper with a purpose in your mind. Use it to read for informative news. Watch only intelligent and knowledge gaining TV programmes. Use your mobile phones only for communication and not for chatting. Use Whatsapp, Facebook and other social media to get connected to people for some specific purpose and not for gossip, time pass etc. By doing these you will feel very calm and peaceful as you distract yourself from negativity and attach yourself only to positivity.

71) Learn to say NO Tactfully

Dare to say NO to leaders who want to get control over you without your consent.

> To say NO tactfully is an art. One has to practice and excel
> in this art.

Bees that have honey in their mouth have stings in their tails. So be careful, stay away and say NO to those people who pretend to be sweet.

Always remember the reality of life is that when you need advice, everyone is ready to help you, but when you need help, everyone is ready to advice you.

72) Make a list of Strengths and Weaknesses

I being a Chartered Accountant by Profession has the habit of making SWOT analysis for any Project/Assignment. We call it Strengths, Weakness, Opportunity and Threat. But in terms of personal life everyone should know their strengths and weaknesses. Every person has its own strength and weakness. No person in this world is living without any weakness. It is the ability of the individual how to show off the strength and capitalize on that and how to cover up and improve weakness. So once you make a list of your strength and weakness, you will be able to work on that. Always remember give maximum time and effort in nurturing and developing your strengths. The more you develop and the more you make your strength stronger, your weakness will slowly and gradually go away. This is like filling the empty glass with water. The more you fill the glass with water vacuum will go away. So follow 80-20 Rule. Give 80% of your effort in increasing your strength and 20% to improve and reduce your weakness. Make your strength strongest and your weakness weakest.

Winners recognize their weaknesses but focus in their strengths. Losers know their strengths but focus on their weaknesses.

Bruce Lee said: "I am not afraid of a fighter who knows a thousand kicks, but I am afraid of the one who has practiced one kick a thousand times."

73) No Pain No Gain

It is a great experience to take risk and challenge as a pain. And the great feeling is to overcome the results of the risk taken. If we take challenges and pain in life, we will learn to win and gain. So be a sport to experiment with situations in life and you will see how easily you become a winner.

It is a scientific law that no mass or energy in this Universe can be destroyed or created. It is just conversion and transformation process. One mass is converted into another mass and one form of energy is transformed into another form. Similarly in life pain is converted into gain and gain is converted into pain. If you take the pain of labor, hard work, sacrifice you get the gain of more money, rewards and recognition. So even for achievement of goal you have to sacrifice something.

No progress can be made and no success can be achieved without facing challenge and struggling against adverse situation and circumstances.

In my school days I learned that Experience is the Best Teacher, but my life taught me that pain is the best teacher because it opened my highway to success. I would have never come School First in my Class X Board exam unless I suffered from two fractures- one in left leg and other in my right hand in a span of 10 months. I tried to overcome that pain by diverting my pain feeling from my fracture to my study by focusing on it. Again when I was bed ridden for more than 6 months when I was suffering from Multi Drug Resistance Tuberculosis, I decided to start alternative career in my wife's name which can give her lifetime income after my death and even in my absence. With the blessings of God my wife Jully Parekh is among the top 10 insurance advisor of Pan India of Birla Sunlife Insurance Co. Ltd. Everything you want is just outside your comfort zone.

You can not get disproportionate gains without disproportionate pain.

74) Make yourself greater than your Problem

We have to rise above our problem to live happily. Whenever we face any problem or difficult situation or circumstances we should encounter it and neutralize it by acting more wisely and thinking more in an enlightened way.

We live on a small planet out of a several million galaxies in this Universe. So are our problems, fear and troubles are bigger than us or are that much serious?? Try to find the solution of any problem from within. Always face your fear/problem boldly. Half of the fear is gone and half the problem is solved if you face it. Never get scared and run away with your fear/problem. Moreover never create imaginary fear and problem. Do all those things from which you have fear or problem to counter and encounter those fear and problem. Very soon you will see that fear is gone and realized that problem is solved. So face fear and problem, counter it and encounter it to kill your fear and problem. Remember life of fear is too short and weak if your confidence is long and strong. This process makes you bigger than your fear and greater than your problem.

The best way to mitigate your problem is not to give it compounding factor to exaggerate or multiply by not telling it to others. This is so because 20% people do not care, 20% show just sympathy, 50% people are glad to know that you have problem and spread it in negative manner and only 10% give attentive listening to your problem to offer some solution and remedy to your problem. So share your problem only with your nearest and dearest people.

In a day when you do not face any problem, be sure that you are travelling on a wrong path. Running away from your problems only increases the distance to the solution.

If you worry about a trouble, it becomes double. But when you smile at it, it disappears like a bubble.

75) Learn and Grow from failure

Learn from failure and rise from failure. No failure is recorded in history of successful man who has never failed and attempted again. The glory is more in doing it again after failure rather than winning trophy. There is nothing like permanent failure. Every failure is a stepping stone to success. Failure teaches us more things like- to be tolerant, to be persistent and patience. Sometimes even we do not know but there is a lesson behind every failure. Failure is a process through which man has to pass to make his destiny. Thank God for having experience of failure and teaching new lesson and giving new strength. Take failures as speed breaker on your path to success. Success achieved after repeated failures last long and forever. Whereas success achieved at one stroke sometimes may be due to luck last for a moment.

The greatest glory in living lies not in never falling but in rising every time we fall. Never confuse a single failure with a final failure.

Success is self explanatory whereas mistakes and failures need explanation. So learn from mistakes and explain yourself the cause of your failure and march again till you achieve success.

Success is the ability to go from one failure to another with no loss of enthusiasm and energy. You have to learn lessons from other's mistakes and failures, because you may get the time to commit all the mistakes yourself.

The man who learns nothing from the past and failure will be punished by the future. The illiterate of then 21st century is not those who can not read and write, but those who can not learn, unlearn and relearn.

Swami Vivekanada said: "One thing I like about stones that come in my way is, once I pass across them, they automatically become my milestone." There are no mistakes, only experiences. There are no problems, only challenges. There are no failures only feedback.

76) Face Change and Challenges with Right Attitude and Open Mind

Always face any changes and challenges with open mind and attitude of acceptance. Never reject or say NO to any change and challenges without understanding it. If the change and challenges are good then accept it willingly. Then express your willingness to adapt/adopt the change and challenge. Then decide to change yourself with it. Lastly do it. So take change and challenge as an option or choice. Keep in mind that the area in which you do not want to change yourself is the area where you need to change. Once you have accepted the change and challenge and ready to adapt/adopt to it, you can follow any of the approaches like physical, mental or spiritual. Whenever you start the process of changing yourself resistance will often come. It may come from outside or from within. But never stop or give up here, because resistance is always good to make better progress. So march ahead and overcome resistance and achieve the goal of changing yourself.

Change and challenge is the natural law of life so always welcome change and challenge with right attitude and open mind. Always face the challenge with a smile and you will realize nothing is impossible.

Change and challenges can be stepping stone or stumbling blocks. It is just a matter of how you take it.

You must be the change, you wish to see in the world. There are two primary choices in life; to accept situation as they exist or accept the responsibility to change the situation.

The ultimate measure of a man is not where he stands in moments of comfort and convenience, but where he stands at times of challenge and controversy. With a bad attitude one can never have a positive day and with a positive attitude one can never have a bad day.

Everyone thinks of changing the world, but no one thinks of himself with the change. A strong and positive attitude creates more miracles.

Life is 10% how you make it and 90% how you take it.

77) Take Help of Trouble shooters

Today's technology has become so advanced and user friendly that whenever you get stuck up, you have the option to click – "HELP", "ASK", "TROUBLE SHOOTER" and get the solution. You can even call on helpline number or just drop a mail for solution to your problem.

Similarly you have to take help of troubleshooters in life if you stuck up. This may be your parents, spouse, brother, sister, mentor, friend or relative whoever is close to you and with whom you can share your problem. Always remember sharing the problem and simply crying with all your tears out solves half of the problem. Sometimes they may give very simple tips which is easy to work on but you failed to recognize it.

Sometimes even watching a good movie with good learning or message act as trouble shooter if you got stuck up in a situation or could not decide what to do in life? I am sharing my experience with you. I am Greatly motivated by Bollywood film "GURU" based on life of Late Dhirubhai Ambani, one of my ideal also. After watching movie I made a dream and made my two goals- one to construct own two storied House and other to own a Mercedes car and with the blessings of God, I achieved both of that well before my target date. Inspired by that movie I made another dream goal of having 100 crore wealth by a certain date. I am working on the plan to achieve that and also made plan how I will use it for myself, my next generation and for the mankind and society as a whole.

78) Avoid Negativity and Deal with Negatives

If you want to remain positive, then you have to eradicate negativity out of your life. This is so because positivity and negativity are like two wives of a single man. A man cannot keep happy both of his wives together in his life. It is said that behind every successful man, there is a woman and behind every failed man, there are more than one woman. So if you want to be successful in your life you have to avoid negativity and deal with negatives to remain positive.

If you have enemies who are trying to pull your life, just tolerate them with a smile and keep your patience and they themselves will fall down into the pitfalls which they dug for you.

Some example to deal with negative thoughts and emotions:

1)   Feel uncomfortable but avoid anger
2)   Get energized but never nervous.
3)   Say I am stretched but not overloaded
4)   See as something different but not terrible.
5)   Feel concerned but never anxious
6)   Try to search but never say lost/gone
7)   Say someone unresourceful but never stupid
8)   Feel overlooked but not rejected
9)   Express excitness instead of scaring
10) Say oops instead of oh!, shit!

You must learn how to avoid detractors, negativity and negatives. An important attribute of successful people is their impatience with negative thinking and negative acting people.

79) Remove Clutters

Clutters means waste of no use. It attracts negative energy. On the other hand, cleanliness is next to Godliness. Clear and clean places gives clear and clean thoughts. You have to remove clutters from:

1) Home, Bathroom, Kitchen
2) Wardrobe, Bed
3) Office
4) Office Tables, Drawers
5) Car
6) Mail Box
7) Mobile SMS
8) Mind (Negative Thoughts, jealousy, ill will etc)
9) Wallet
10) Your Office bag/Briefcase.

Create space for new things. Remove all those things which you have not used it for a single time in last 12 months. Sell it, give it away or burn it but get rid of it.

80) Brainstorming and Servicing

Brain is the CPU of human body. We should maintain it healthy and service it regularly. I would call this AMC of Mental House. We should regularly clean our mind with negative thoughts and beliefs and messages. I would advise the following steps to follow to make mental house cleaning and servicing regularly.

1. Sit down with pen and paper at least once in a year with yourself only
2. Note down all negative thought, belief, message came to you or any bad experience with the following person:

   i.   From / with your parents
   ii.   From / with your spouse
   iii. From / with your children
   iv.   From / with your relatives
   v.   From / with your business partner
   vi.   From / with your clients/customers
   vii. From / with your mentors/gurus/teachers
   viii. From / with your friends
   ix.   From / with your charismatic personality/celebrity
   x.   From / with your within

Try to find out the root cause of that belief, thought, message or bad experience. By doing these, feel that you have taken out all those belief, negative thoughts, message and experience from your mind on that piece of paper and then tear it off that paper into tiny pieces and throw it into dust bin or burn it. Your mind is fully clean and serviced.

81) Read Impossible as I M Possible

Some people see things and events and ask- How, Why or say amazing, beautiful, unbelievable etc. If you want to stand out in a crowd as an extraordinary then dream of things and events and goal that never were there and ask – Why Not?, Why Impossible??. Then reply your question by saying loudly yes – "I can do it". "I will do it", "I will make it possible".

You can make slogan of your life or your mission statement- "Impossible means I M Possible." Never believe in limitations because we live in limit less Universe with infinite resources.

The slogan for my life is "I believe in Infinity".

The best way to make impossible things possible is to start doing it. It is said that wisdom is knowing what to do, skill is knowing how to do but the quality is doing it. If you start doing what you know with the help of your skill, it is for sure to make something possible which looks impossible before doing it. The smallest action is always better than powerful thought. It is only by doing one can know whether it is possible or impossible. In other words, give more importance to action after making necessary planning and thinking. It is only the action which converts plans into reality. It is only your action gives your plans and thoughts a physical existence. That is why it is said that everything is created twice in this world. Convert your thoughts into words and convert your words into action and make action your habit because action conquers fear and when fear is gone, you have the power to read Impossible as I M Possible.

Difficult things take a long time; the impossible takes a little longer. Impossible is not a fact, it is an opinion.

82) Overcome Problems to get Benefits

If problem cannot be solved, then why to worry.

If problem can be solved then what is need to worry. So if there is a genuine problem at all, there is nothing to do but there is always something to know to solve the problem. Hence take problem as an opportunity to learn and then get to know and understand that learning and then solve the problem with learning and finally get benefits by overcoming problem.

Always think about the benefits you will get by solving the problem. Never make your problems more problematic by thinking that how difficult it is to solve the problem. This is based on the Law if Attraction. The more you think about problem, your problem will get bigger and exaggerated. The more you think about benefit, more solution will come into your mind to solve the problem.

Almost all problems can be solved if they are stated well. First write down your problem in detail on a piece of paper. Second break down your problem into smallest of the smallest parts. Third take out that part of the problem which affects everyone including you because you have to do very little about that. Fourth rearrange those parts of the problem which affect you only or special to you. Fifth identify the factors, causes and reasons for each small part of your problem which affect you only. Sixth find a solution for those factors, causes and reasons.

You may have dreams and you may have problems. Overcome your problems to make your dream true. Obstacles are those frightful things you see when you take your eyes off your goal.

Problems and difficulties do not come to destroy you but to help you realize your hidden potential. Let difficulties and problems know that you are also strong and tough. Successful people think about solutions most of the time. unsuccessful people think about problems and difficulties most of the time.

83) Save for rainy day

This is the most important activity we have to do regularly and in a disciplined manner. It sounds a very simple advice

People say you have to keep at least 1-3 month savings in your bank as contingency fund to meet an emergency. If keeping such amount separately allocating it is difficult than I would suggest to build that fund by piggy bank

Deposit daily Rs100-500 in that box and whatever amount is accumulated at the end of the month deposit into bank. Do this exercise regularly for one year and after that you may reduce the daily amount but never leave this habit

This is a simple financial exercise and follow it religiously.

Never save what is left after spending. Always spend what is left after savings. Make savings a priority over spending. Invest what you have saved in different baskets as per your needs, contingencies and goals.

Beware of little expenses. A small leak can sink a large ship. It is of no use to carry an umbrella if your shoes are leaking.

If you are born poor, it is not your mistake, but if you die poor is your mistake, said by Bill Gates.

84) Control your expenses and monitor your income

Maintain records of your daily expenses and sum it up for the month. Divide your monthly expenses into four categories:

1. Essential for basic necessity
2. Needed for comfort
3. Avoidable or postponed
4. Wastege or unnecessary

On the basis of the above make budget for the yearly expenses and at the end of the year compare it with actual

Similarly, maintain record of monthly income and sum it up for the year. Divide your yearly income into four categories

1. recurring salary or business income
2. Intreast, rental or Royalty income
3. Surplus arise on sale of assets/investments
4. casual or non-recovering or wind fall income

On the basis of the above forecast your income for the next 5-10 years in consonance with your financial goals.
Borrow only in do or die situation as borrower becomes the lender's slave.
Never buy things you don't need else you will have to sell things you need.
Have multiple source of income.

Too many people spend money they have not earned, to buy things they do not want, to impress people they do not like, just to satisfy his ego and make other people jealous. Allocate 70% of your budget on your necessity, 20% on your comfort and 10% on your luxury.

85) Set your financial plan for a decade

Very poor people plan for a day
Poor people plan for a week
Middle class people plan for a month
Rich people plan for a year
Very rich plan for a decade
So, set your financial goal for a decade and follow it.
Follow the formula: Income – savings/investment =expenses
And not: Income – expenses=savings/investment

Remember to achieve freedom in life financial security is must, must and must

Financial planning is necessary in following areas:

1. Having children when and how much
2. Education and higher education and marriage of children
3. Retirement
4. Home, car and other tangibles
5. Holidays/vacations charity and other intangibles
6. Protection of life and tangibles
7. Contingency and emergency

Financial planning should be carried on with the help of experts. It should be reviewed periodically with respect to age and goals.

I would suggest to read and follow my book "Golden Rules of Money Making". It explains how to get rich, stay rich and die rich.

Always remember finance is the backbone of any business. Money in life is like blood in our body. If money flows freely then our financial health will be healthy. I believe that money is not God but not lesser than God. Bless your money whenever you give it or receive it. Make yourself financially disciplined.

People always overestimate what they can do in one year but always under estimate what they can do in 5 or 10 years.

D) Spiritual and Humanity Life Management

86) Give something to the world

The world will remember you if you have given something to it. The world will never remember for whatever you made for you or however big you are. Service to humanity is a noble cause. It is said Mahatma Gandhi attained the highest level of humanity only by serving the society and spending his life till death for noble cause for a country at large. In fact the essence of all religion is also a service to humanity.

The best way to give something to anybody is not to expect anything from anyone. Make a habit of doing at least one activity a month for someone in which you give your love without any expectation or anything in return.

We just cannot eat the fruits. We must become the tree one day.

The highest form of religion is doing something for others. Out of 720 hours in a month spend around 720 minutes for humanity, society and social service.

Always follow Newton's Third Law of Motion: "To every action there is an equal and opposite reaction." to make your life very simple. In other words, you get back what you give to this world. Life is an 'Echo'. What you send out- comes back.

We got the right only to give to this world as we cannot take away anything from this world. Life is an echo, it all comes back. The good, the bad, the false, the true. So give the world the best you have and the best will come back to you. Give more and you will have more. A candle loses nothing of its light by lighting another candle. There are two kinds of people in the world: Givers and Takers. The takers may eat better, but the givers sleep better. To give service to the society by a single heart by some act is better than a thousand heads bowing in prayer.

87) Do something new and wonderful

Daily do something new and wonderful, at least one of the following:

1. Meet at least one new person
2. Do at least one new thing you have never done
3. Go to at least one new or unknown place
4. Eat at least one new food you never ate before.

By doing so you will come closer and closer to God because God created you for two reason:

1. To create new for this world and/or
2. To explore this world

While doing something new and wonderful, the world will doubt you so believe in yourself and doubt the world to do something new and wonderful.

An idea has a limited shelf life. Act on it. If you cannot act on your idea, share it with others. Do not let your idea die.

Whenever you go out for recreation weekly or go for outing every year, you should re-create something out of that holiday or vacation. It will be your effective recreation if you re-create something that give peace to your soul. An outer body cannot improve the soul but if you improve your soul then your body will automatically improve. It is very important to live happily to re-create your soul and body out of recreation. It will give new sense to your soul and your body will get fresh energy. It connects you with yourself and then to ultimate God.

If you do what you have always done, you will get what you have always got. Do what you can, with what you have.

88) Forget the Past, Live in the Present

Past often makes you sad, Future increases your anxiety but the present gives you power. Man feels anxious when he is living in the future and he feels depressed when he is living in the past.

You will find in majority of investment schemes it is written in small letters "Past performance or returns is just an indicator, not a guarantee or assurance." Similarly in life past success does not guarantee future success and also past failure does not stamp on you that you are a failure forever. So forget the past bad or good, live in now and present and plan and think positive for future. Make up your Now to show your Tomorrow. Never feel guilty for the past because nobody can change it.

The source of most of our frustrations and anxiety are the result of living in the future or the past. The best time to plant a tree was 20 years back; the second best time is today.

Feeling sorry for yourself, and your present condition, is not only a waste of energy but the worst habit you could possibly have. We can not have a better tomorrow and future if we are thinking about yesterday and the past all the time.

Mission of Osho: My whole effort is to pull my people away from the past and the future and just make them available to the intense beauty of the present.

89) Live Today as your Last Day of Life Learn Today as your First Day of School

I do not believe in deferred happiness. I do not store today's happiness for tomorrow.

Treasure every moment. Yesterday is history, tomorrow is mystery, Today is the Gift, That is why it is called the Present.

Today is the present and understand the power of Present. The more you live in the present, the more you live in Now, the more you are living your Life.

Live your today to the fullest assuming there is no tomorrow. Just live your life today and give your best for today. Similarly take all learning's seriously and learn it as ABCD 0r 123 as if you are going to school today for the first time.

One of the greatest enemies that we can ever face in life is, illusion that there will be more time tomorrow than today.

90) Never ask what you Want, Never complain what you don't have BUT appreciate for what you have to GOD

The Universe is infinite. The God has created everything in this Universe for us. So feel abundance in life and thank God for whatever you have. Never complain but rather express your gratitude to God in advance for the things that will come in your life. Also never ask from God but rather convey message that you are going to get certain things from him in future and say thanks in advance. Never feel scarcity. Always get satisfaction and be happy with what you have, what you are and where you are. This only means that you should not curse anyone for what you do not have and get jealousy by seeing others with what they have. It does not stop you from dreaming and sending positive vibrations to nature for what you want.

Make a Gratitude of Thank You book. Start writing thank you and express your gratitude and appreciate God for at least one good experience of yours in a day. This seems very simple task but sometimes very simple task is very difficult to do or implement it as an habit. So start this as an habit because God also likes appreciation and receiving thanks sent with love and with true heart just as we feel happy whenever anyone appreciate us.

We can not have all that we desire, but we will get all that we deserve.

91) Ultimate happiness and its source

Jesus Christ said "The best way to get happiness is to make others happy."
It is the price we are paying to the Nature and effort we are making for making others happy in turn to nature's effort to give us happiness.

Happiness and money is the ultimate goal and objective of life. Happiness can be attained and money can be retained only by making others happy and by showing generosity in life.

I would say money grows on tree. If you sow the seed of quality service to humanity and mankind, you can reap crop, fruits and flowers of money.

We all are labors and workmen of God. So God will pay handsome salary to those who are skilled, industrious and highly competent and efficient in rendering service to humanity and mankind.

Showing compassion empathy and sympathy towards the person suffering some pain or in trouble and trying to help them can bring true happiness to your life. Moreover this happiness will last forever.

Happiness is not based on external status. It is an internal status.

The key to happiness is not that you never get angry, upset, frustrated, irritated or depressed, it is how fast you get out of all these nonsense.

92) What is life??

Life is an Adventure, Dare it
Life is a Beauty, Praise it
Life is a Challenge, Meet it
Life is a Duty, Perform it
Life is Eternal, Make it Divine
Life is a Friendship, Hold it
Life is a Gift, Accept it
Life is a Game, Play it
Life is an Honesty, Make it Policy
Life is Interesting, Make it
Life is a Journey, Complete it
Life is Kindness, Show it
Life is Love, Enjoy it
Life is Mystery, Unfold it
Life is Noble, Do it
Life is Opportunity, Grab it
Life is Puzzle, Solve it
Life is Promise, Fulfill it
Life is Quiz, Answer it
Life is Risky, Take it
Life is Sorrow, Overcome it
Life is a Song, Sing it
Life is Spirit, Realize it
Life is Struggle, Fight it
Life is Tragedy, Face it
Life is Victory, Share it

93) What is in a Life??

Best Day, Today
Biggest Mistake, Waste of Time
Biggest Obstacle, Speak More, Listen Less
Worst Thought, Jealousy
Best Mentor, One who Inspires
Most Wise Person, Listens All But does What his Heart Says
Worst Habit, To Blame/Curse/Gossip
Valuable Wealth, Education
Valuable Donation, Blood Donation
Best Time, NOW
Best Friend, Stand by us All the Time
Best Habit, To Forgive
Best Thought, Positive Thought
Best Show, Show Kindness
Best thing to Increase, Your Reputation
Best Thing to Decrease, Conflict and Controversy
Best thing to Manage, Money
Best To do for anyone, Prayer

94) Earn Name. Fame and Status Follows

Many people struggle for fame and work hard for status and win it and it all lost into realm of silence when death comes. Nothing exists out of that. But the name we have earned with the help of our nature, our acts and deeds of humanity and kindness, extending helping hand and showing the way to the needy people will remain forever even after our death. That is one of the most precious and valuable treasure among others which we are leaving behind. People will remember our Name. So feel legacy with your Name.

95) Make a Prayer of Gratitude Everyday

Prayer is the food for soul so everyday make a Prayer to God.
"I am one of those created by Almighty God.

He has given me all the powers to create my own life.

I am thankful to God that I am living.

I am thankful to God that all good and positive things are coming into my life.

I am thankful to God that I can see and feel the Nature and enjoying in this Universe. I am thankful to God that I am living my life with all power and full confidence.

I am thankful to God that every day I am marching towards my goal and purpose in life.

I am thankful to God that I am able to find time for myself, my family and for my relatives and friends.

I am thankful to God that I am full of energy and ready to face all situations in my life.

I am thankful to God that I can feel love, happiness and affluence in my life.

I am thankful to God that I am free from all bonding and enjoying freedom in my life.

I am thankful to God that I am complete and accept myself.

I am Thankful to God that I am part of it so I am also perfect like Almighty."

The best religion is that act with good intention, do good for self and others and feel good. Of all the 'attitudes' we can acquire, surely the attitude of gratitude is the most important and by far the most life changing.

96) Stay connected with 5 elements of Nature to Connect with God

It is said that our body is made up of 5 elements of Nature- Earth, water, Air, Fire and Sky. Even after death our body get mixed into these 5 elements and our soul is set free. So involve with these 5 elements and make deep observation of it and attach yourself with it. If you remain connected with all these it will be very easy to connect with yourself and then to ultimate with God. To stay connected with Nature in your everyday life you can do the following:

1. Sit on the floor of your house at least for half an hour daily either watching TV, reading newspaper or take your meal sitting on the ground.
2. Drink water kept in earthenware pot instead of mineral water or refrigerated water
3. Sit in open air or under a fan instead of sitting in AC room
4. Go out in open air and walk for some time in day time or morning time under the Sun or take Sun Bath occasionally.
5. Watch the night sky from window or go to terrace and look into the sky and see moon and try to count stars and feel the abundance of Nature and Universe.

Mahatma Gandhi said: "When I admire the wonders of a sunset or the beauty of the Moon, my soul expands in worship of the Creator."

97) Conflict Management

Conflict can never be settled with anger. It can also be never permanently settled by war or by killing. If we settle in this manner we may get peace temporary as powerful subdues the weak, but the sense of wrong will remain in weak, the fire of revenge will gather wind and will broke out one day. In other words it will become more furious and sometimes run from generation to generation.

The best way to manage conflict is either to surrender or runaway from the situation and then revisit the situation placing each party into other party's shoes and analyze the situation calmly. If you feel it is your mistake then go and say sorry to the other person and if you find other person was at bigger fault then also go to him and say that you could not understand him and show sympathy.

At the end, I wish all conflict should cease, all hostility be removed and spreading the love and care everywhere because that is all humanity.

Write down the names of at least five people with you want to improve your relation in next five months. Plan how to do this.

98) Serve Poor and Needy People

Changing your life is a good start.

Changing the world will be a good end.

Show compassions to poor and needy persons. Measure yourself by how much you do for poor and needy people and the society will measure you by your noble deeds and contribution.

My heart beats and with every beat it silently tells me, I am worth the beat. And so I promised to my heart, I will make a difference to myself and to the world.

For a person who is willing to serve before trying to get reward finds endless, numerous and abundant opportunities in this world to serve poor and needy persons and contribute to society.

I am a member of networking organization Business Network International (BNI) which runs on the philosophy "Giver's Gain".

History is the proof that no person in the world is popular or famous or people still remember them by how much money he has made. But one can become popular or famous or people will remember them by their contribution to society and by service to humanity or mankind. Take example of Mahatma Gandhi or Mother Teresa.

Show your kindness, express your gratitude, offer your help to every person you see and meet who is in need of any of these. Achieving success or doing some great act may put your name in limelight or in some newspaper or your photo with interview may come in some magazine or your video may come in You tube, but this is all temporary. But if you helped a poor family by providing right education to their children or offered a job for earning member of any poor family, then you will be remembered forever. Even if you do a small act of kindness everyday as your habit, it will accumulate and gets compounded and it will be enough to make your life eternal when you die. You must not lose faith in humanity. Humanity is an ocean; if a few drops of the ocean are dirty, the ocean does not become dirty.

99) Donate Before you Die

As we earn and spend and pay taxes to Government, similarly you should donate a part of your earnings regularly. You can make small donation everyday or a specific amount every month or a lump sum amount at the end of a year. But make it an habit. Donate for any noble cause which you think and believe is right and appropriate. Giving/sharing/donating makes your soul rich and you will feel divine. The satisfaction you get from donating is very much eternal and unexplainable. It is not necessary that you should make only monetary contribution. You can also get involved and take active participation physically in any charitable and social activities or attaching yourself with any charitable organization on honorary and serve the society by providing your knowledge and skill.

Also donate a portion of your wealth before you die for a noble cause. Even the richest of the richest person like Bill Gates, Warren Buffet have done this and some of them are also actively engaged in social activities.

Always remember Locker facility is not available in Coffins.

By donating you will never feel regret in your life, by helping a poor family by providing education to their child or offering a job to the earning member of that family, you will understand the importance of family, by attending the funeral of your enemy, you will understand the meaning of death and forgiveness. Once you understand all these, then you are not only learning how to live but also how to die rich with eternal wealth

Everyone knows how to count but very few knows what counts.

100) Life is Journey, Enjoy it and Complete it

Treat Life as a journey and the destination is same for all. So enjoy the journey and never rush to reach the destination.

Remember if we enjoy our journey and remain happy all the time, we feel great when we reach the destination and feel fresh to enjoy the beauty of the new place and destination.

Similarly in our life we have to remain happy all the time by living in present and enjoy every moment of it to enjoy the fruits of your goal when you achieve it. Always maintain a balance between living in present and achieving your goals in future.

To reach our ultimate destination, we all travel on different roads. Some roads are smooth and easy whereas some are rough and tough. Every one has to face some hurdles and some speed breakers. So to face these hurdles and to overcome it has become part of life. We have to detach ourselves from the result or outcome of every experience to make ourselves happy. If you go to a hill station you can see both mountains and valley at the same time.

I have learned a little bit of Neuro Linguistic Programming (NLP) and as per TOTE model of NLP, there are no results but only feedback for every input. It is up to us to choose the feedback and convert it into output. Similarly I believe in life there are only feedback but no failures, no tragedy but only event as per God's wish, no problem but new thing to learn.

I believe in just living life happily with every heart beat and with every breathe we take.

LIVE LIFE TO THE FULLEST OF JOY AND HAPPINESS.

I would like to end with the wordings of Swami Vivekananda, "Man wishes to fly like a bird, sing like cuckoo, dance like a peacock, swim like a fish, but man does not wish to live life like a man."